GW01311394

THIS BOOK BELONGS TO:

Date:

Departure Location	Departure Time
Stopover	Time
Arrival Location	Date & Time

Weather
Wind
Forecast
Visibility
Wave

Course / Coordinates
Speed
Distance
Crew

Sketch	Notes

Photo

Anecdotes / Special Moments

Route

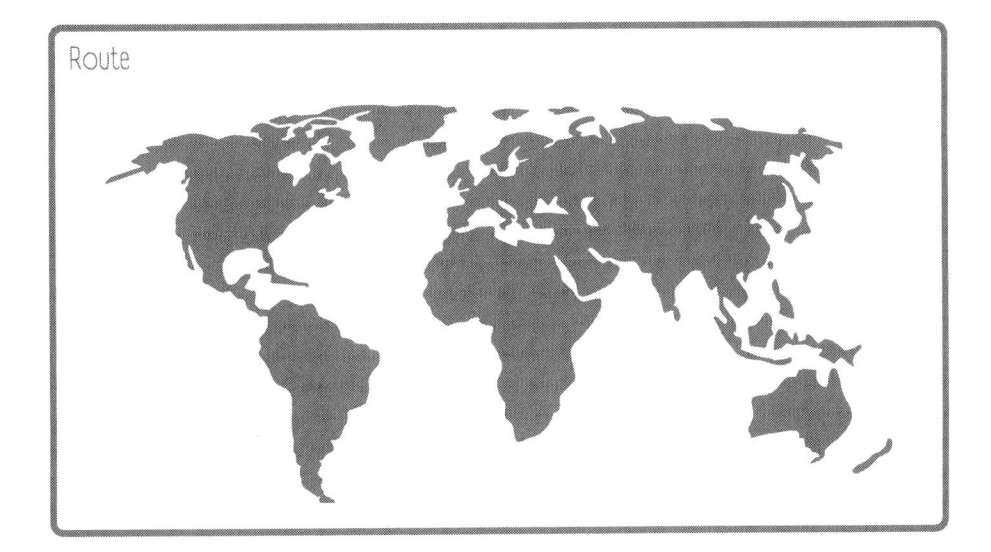

Date:

Departure Location	Departure Time
Stopover	Time
Arrival Location	Date & Time

Weather	
Wind	
Forecast	
Visibility	
Wave	

Course / Coordinates	
Speed	
Distance	
Crew	

Sketch	Notes

Anecdotes / Special Moments

Route

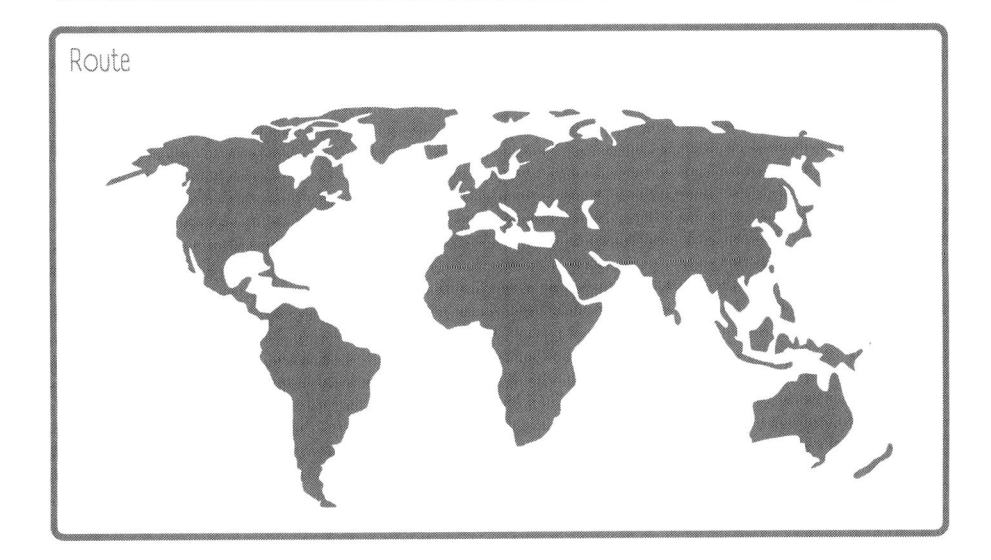

Date:

Departure Location	Departure Time
Stopover	Time
Arrival Location	Date & Time

Weather
Wind
Forecast
Visibility
Wave

Course / Coordinates
Speed
Distance
Crew

Sketch	Notes

Photo

Anecdotes / Special Moments

Route

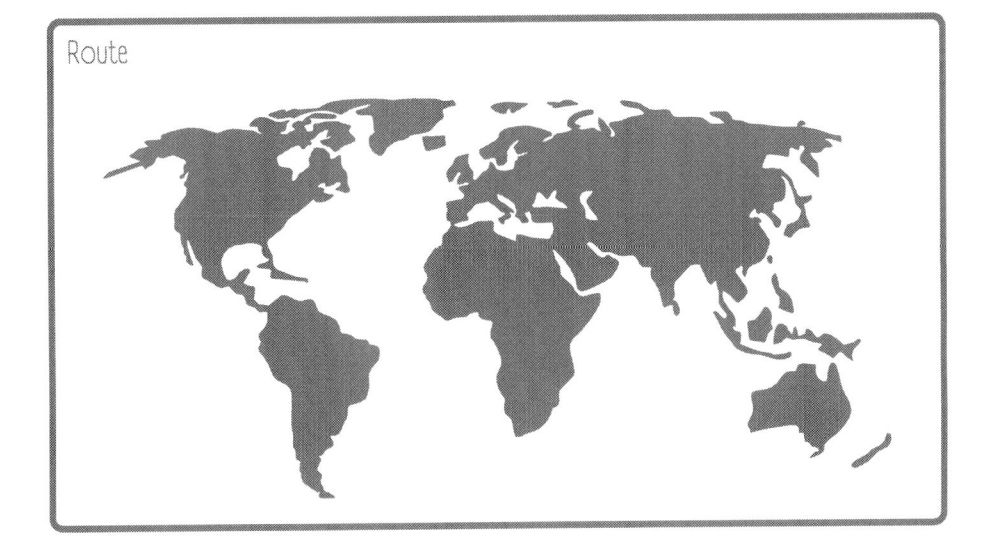

Date: ....

Departure Location	Departure Time
Stopover	Time
Arrival Location	Date & Time

Weather
Wind
Forecast
Visibility
Wave

Course / Coordinates
Speed
Distance
Crew

Sketch	Notes

Photo

Anecdotes / Special Moments

Route

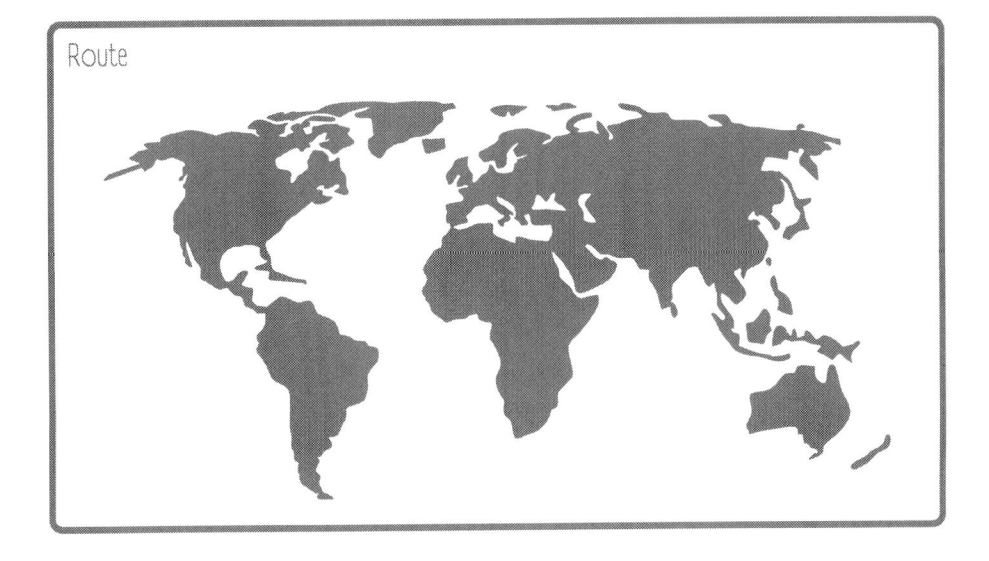

Date:

Departure Location	Departure Time
Stopover	Time
Arrival Location	Date & Time

Weather
Wind
Forecast
Visibility
Wave

Course / Coordinates
Speed
Distance
Crew

Sketch	Notes

Photo

Anecdotes / Special Moments

Route

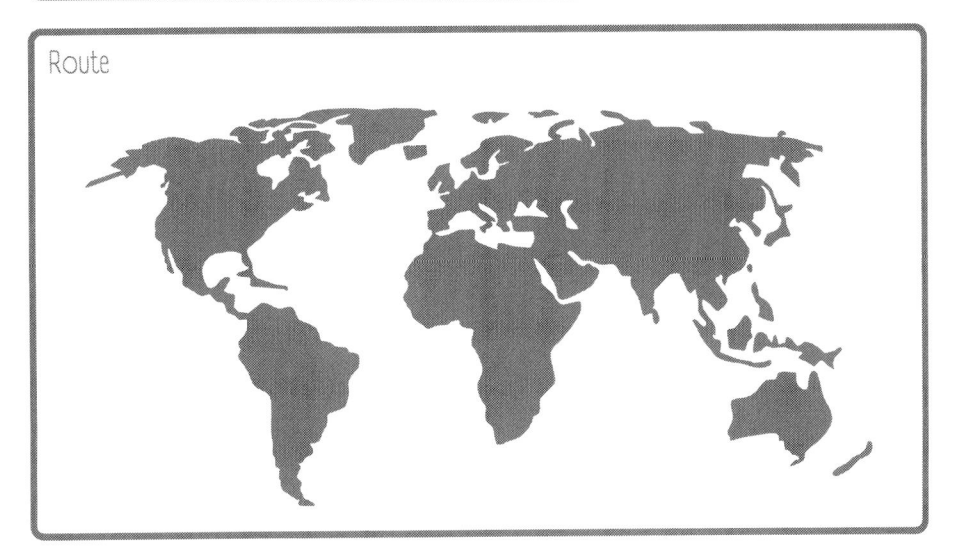

Date:

Departure Location	Departure Time
Stopover	Time
Arrival Location	Date & Time

Weather
Wind
Forecast
Visibility
Wave

Course / Coordinates
Speed
Distance
Crew

Sketch	Notes

Photo

Anecdotes / Special Moments

Route

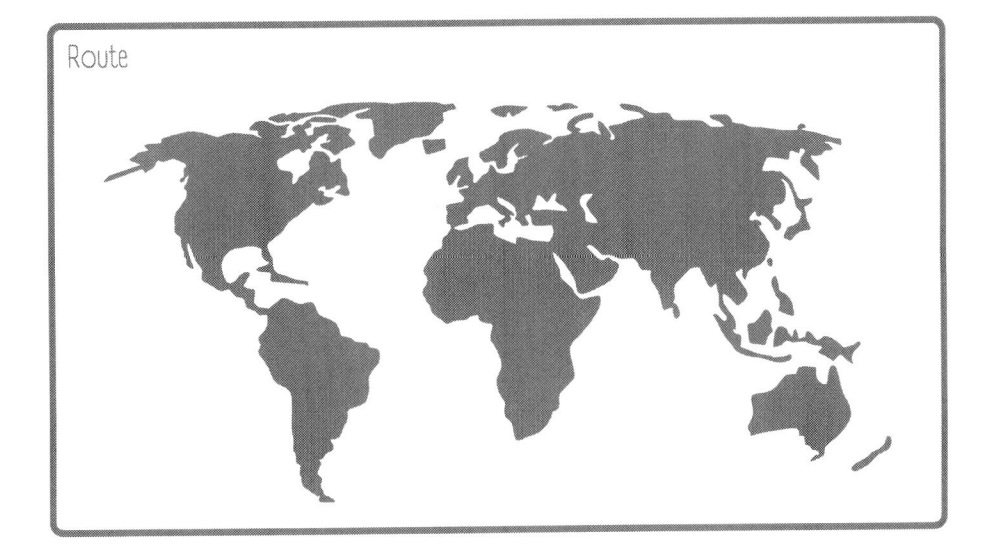

Date:

Departure Location	Departure Time
Stopover	Time
Arrival Location	Date & Time

Weather
Wind
Forecast
Visibility
Wave

Course / Coordinates
Speed
Distance
Crew

Sketch	Notes

Photo

Anecdotes / Special Moments

Route

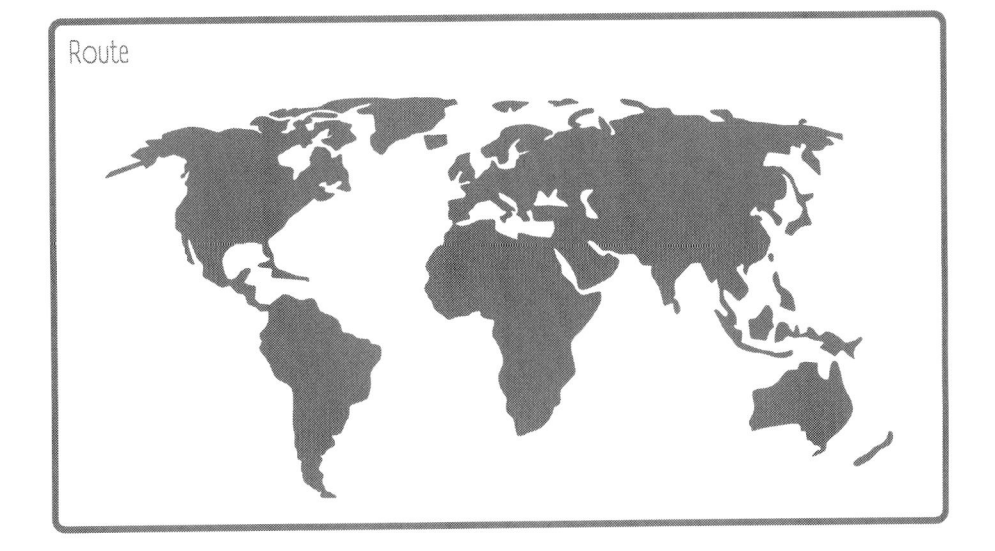

Date:

Departure Location		Departure Time
Stopover		Time
Arrival Location		Date & Time

Weather
Wind
Forecast
Visibility
Wave

Course / Coordinates
Speed
Distance
Crew

Sketch	Notes

Photo

Anecdotes / Special Moments

Route

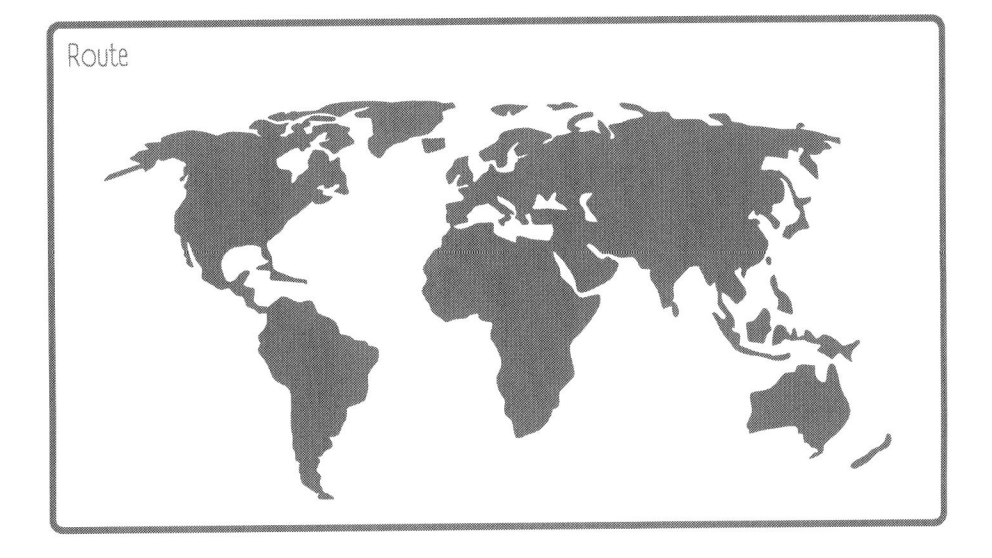

Date: ....

Departure Location	Departure Time
Stopover	Time
Arrival Location	Date & Time

Weather
Wind
Forecast
Visibility
Wave

Course / Coordinates
Speed
Distance
Crew

Sketch	Notes

Photo

Anecdotes / Special Moments

Route

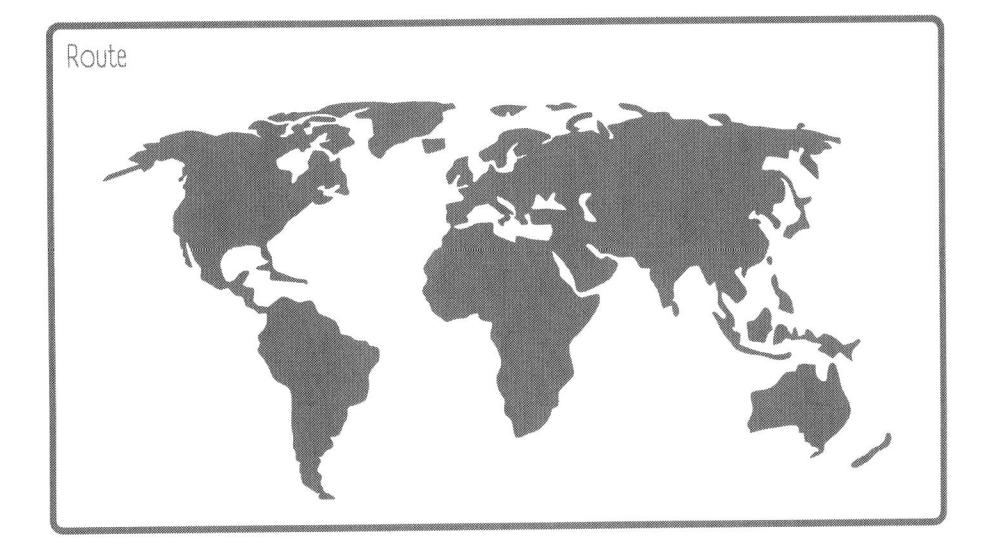

Date: ....

Departure Location	Departure Time
Stopover	Time
Arrival Location	Date & Time

Weather
Wind
Forecast
Visibility
Wave

Course / Coordinates
Speed
Distance
Crew

Sketch	Notes

Photo

Anecdotes / Special Moments

Route

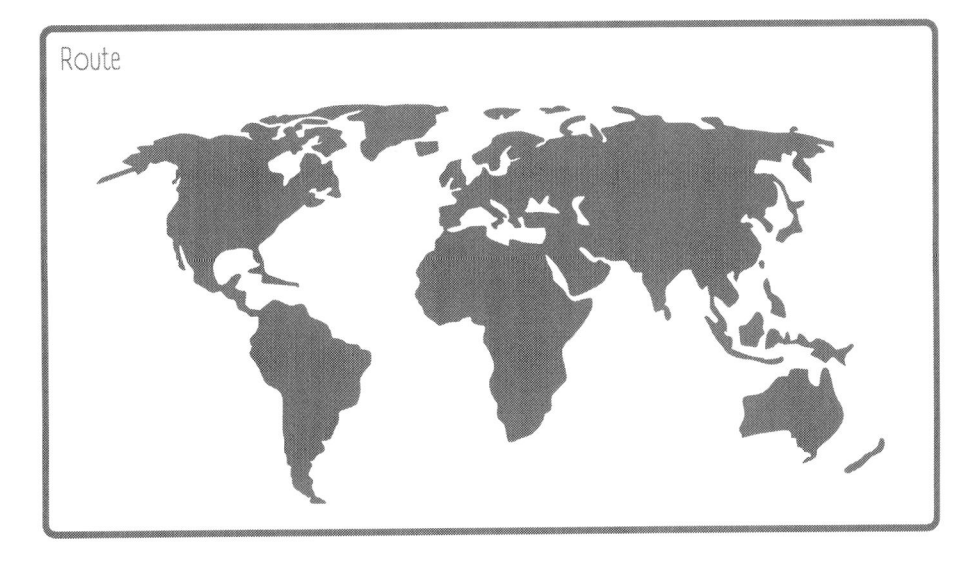

Date: ....

Departure Location	Departure Time
Stopover	Time
Arrival Location	Date & Time

Weather	
Wind	
Forecast	
Visibility	
Wave	

Course / Coordinates	
Speed	
Distance	
Crew	

Sketch	Notes

Photo

Anecdotes / Special Moments

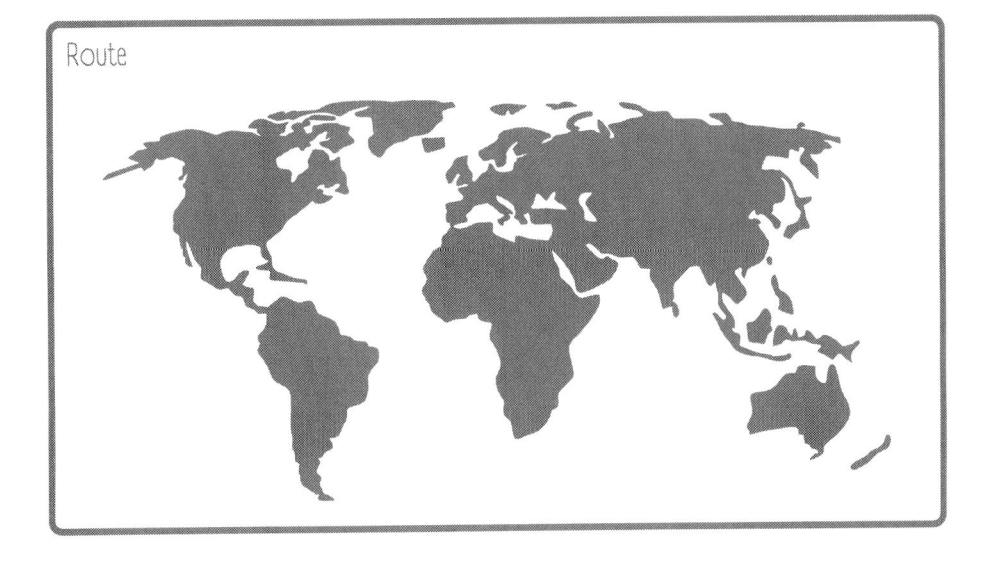

Route

Date: ....

Departure Location	Departure Time
Stopover	Time
Arrival Location	Date & Time

Weather
Wind
Forecast
Visibility
Wave

Course / Coordinates
Speed
Distance
Crew

Sketch	Notes

Photo

Anecdotes / Special Moments

Route

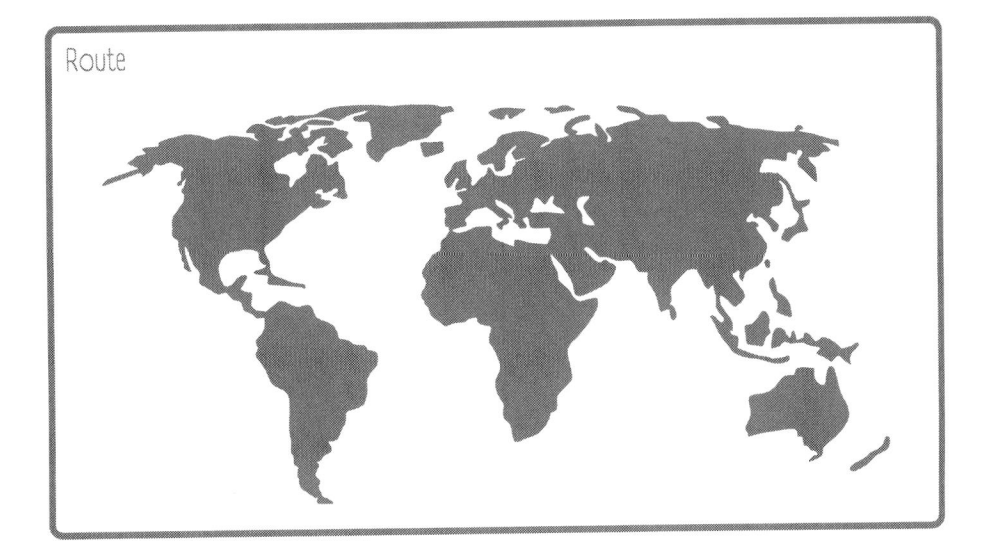

Date:

Departure Location		Departure Time
Stopover		Time
Arrival Location		Date & Time

Weather
Wind
Forecast
Visibility
Wave

Course / Coordinates
Speed
Distance
Crew

Sketch	Notes

Photo

Anecdotes / Special Moments

Route

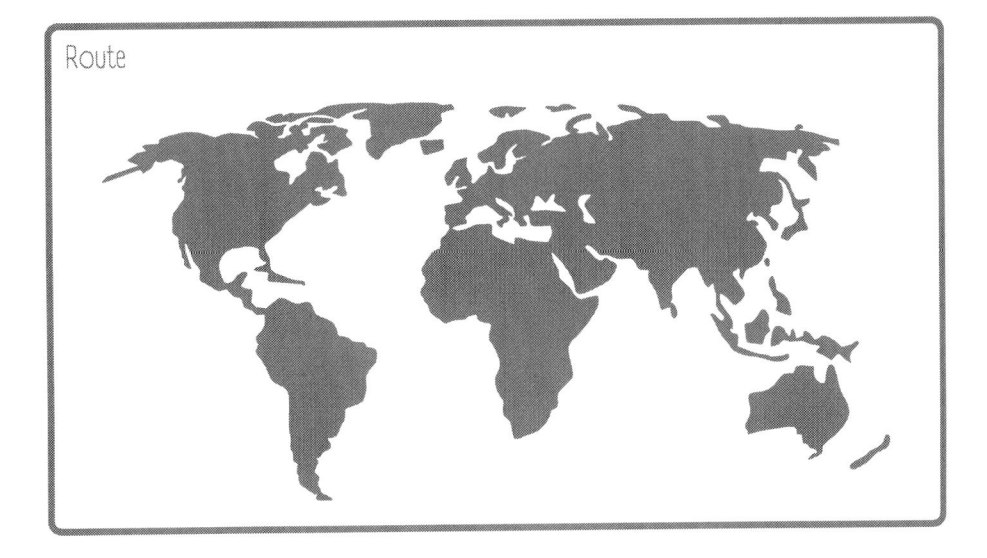

Date: ....

Departure Location	Departure Time
Stopover	Time
Arrival Location	Date & Time

Weather
Wind
Forecast
Visibility
Wave

Course / Coordinates
Speed
Distance
Crew

Sketch	Notes

Photo

Anecdotes / Special Moments

Route

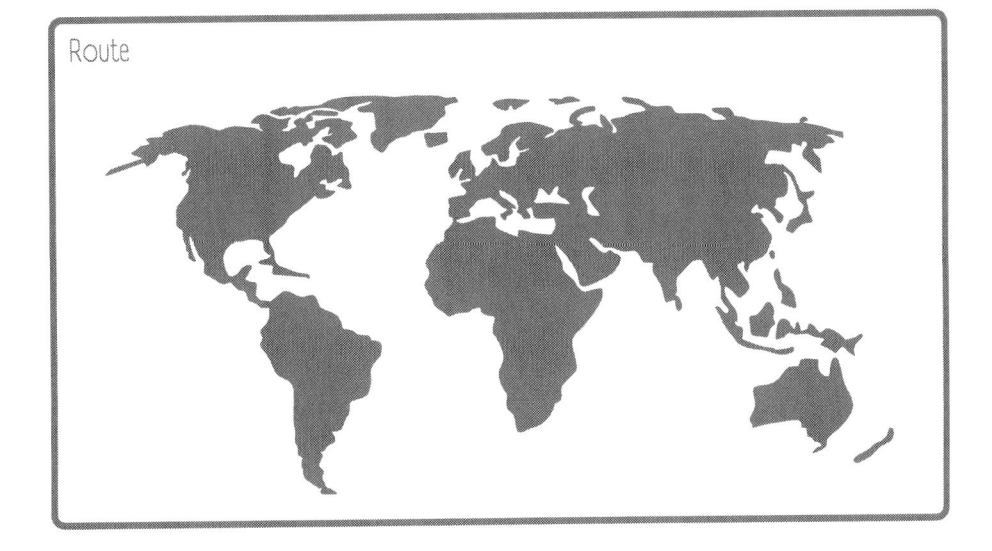

Date: ....

Departure Location	Departure Time
Stopover	Time
Arrival Location	Date & Time

Weather	
Wind	
Forecast	
Visibility	
Wave	

Course / Coordinates	
Speed	
Distance	
Crew	

Sketch	Notes

Photo

Anecdotes / Special Moments

Route

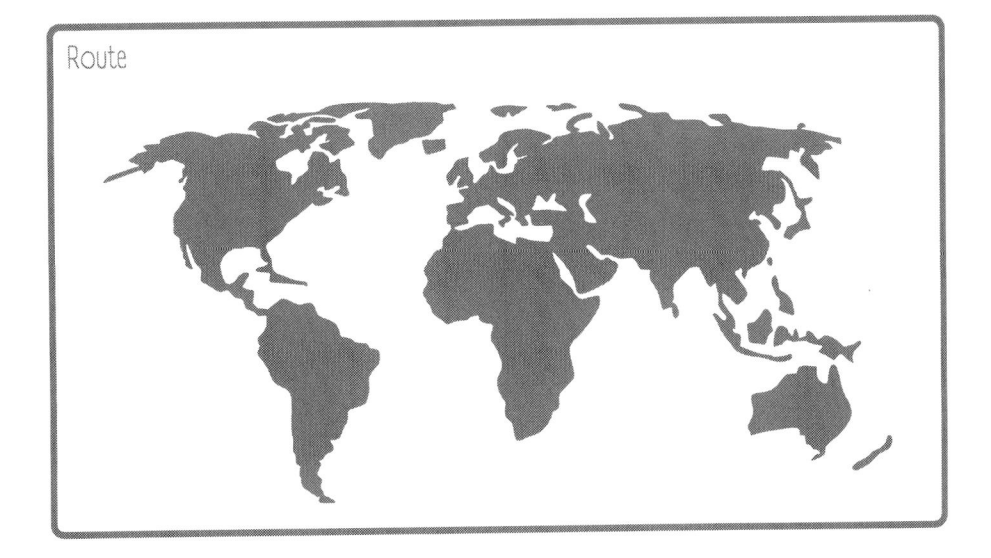

Date:

Departure Location	Departure Time
Stopover	Time
Arrival Location	Date & Time

Weather	
Wind	
Forecast	
Visibility	
Wave	

Course / Coordinates	
Speed	
Distance	
Crew	

Sketch	Notes

Photo

Anecdotes / Special Moments

Route

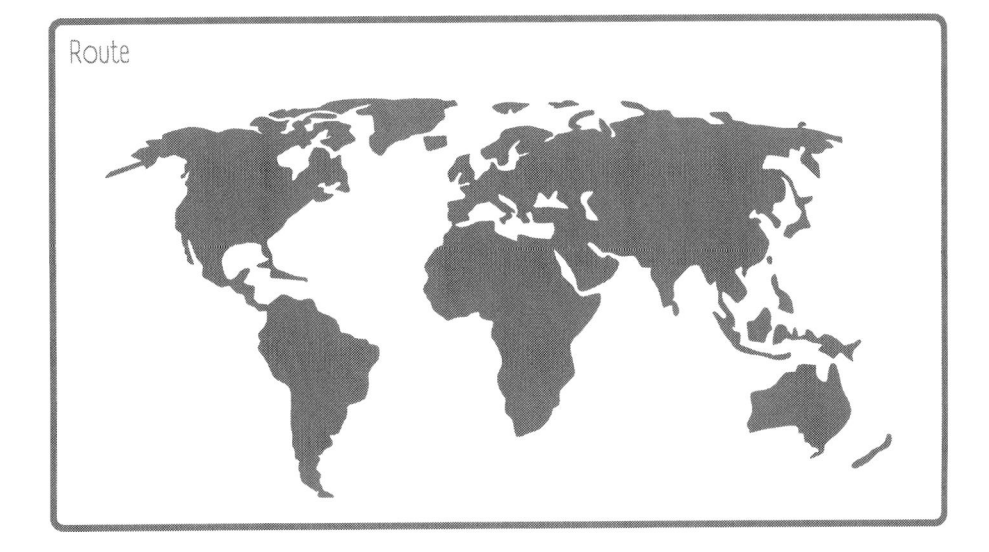

Date:

Departure Location	Departure Time
Stopover	Time
Arrival Location	Date & Time

Weather	
Wind	
Forecast	
Visibility	
Wave	

Course / Coordinates	
Speed	
Distance	
Crew	

Sketch	Notes

Photo

Anecdotes / Special Moments

Route

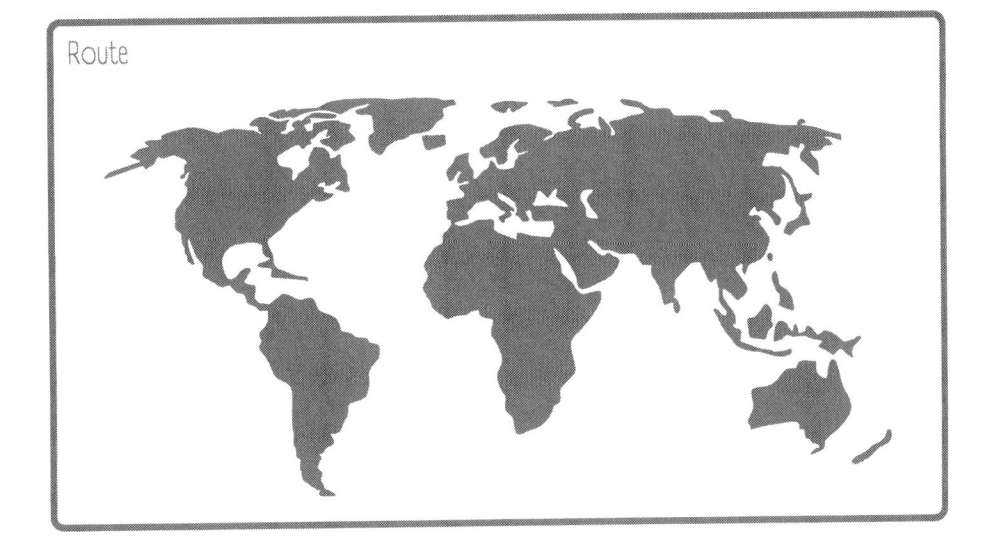

Date:

Departure Location	Departure Time
Stopover	Time
Arrival Location	Date & Time

Weather
Wind
Forecast
Visibility
Wave

Course / Coordinates
Speed
Distance
Crew

Sketch	Notes

Photo

Anecdotes / Special Moments

Route

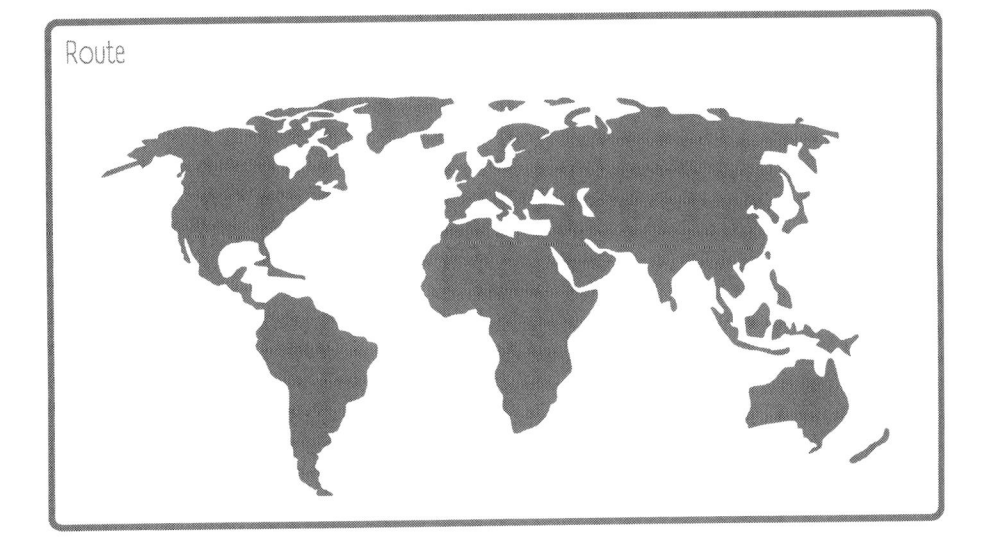

Date:

Departure Location	Departure Time
Stopover	Time
Arrival Location	Date & Time

Weather	
Wind	
Forecast	
Visibility	
Wave	

Course / Coordinates	
Speed	
Distance	
Crew	

Sketch	Notes

Anecdotes / Special Moments

Route

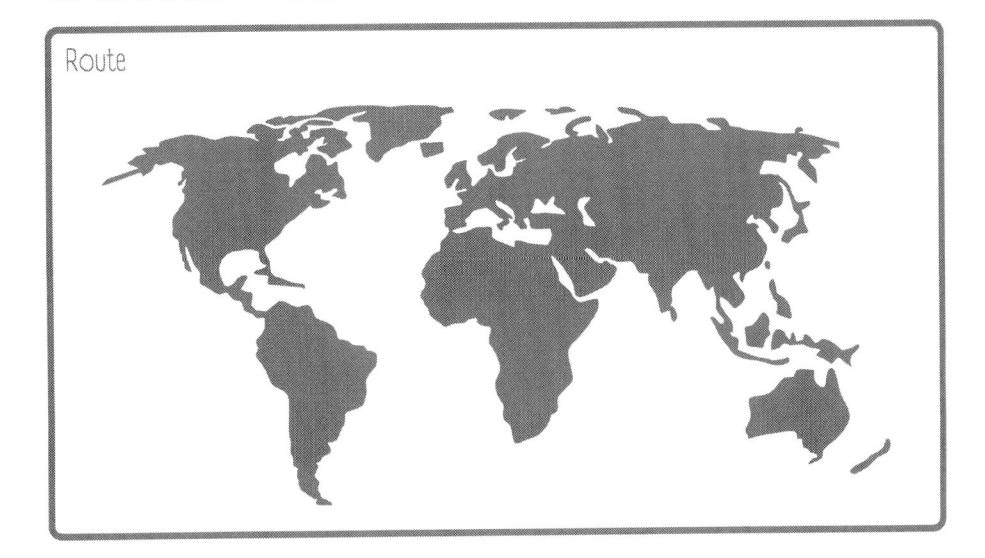

Date:

Departure Location	Departure Time
Stopover	Time
Arrival Location	Date & Time

Weather	
Wind	
Forecast	
Visibility	
Wave	

Course / Coordinates	
Speed	
Distance	
Crew	

Sketch	Notes

Photo

Anecdotes / Special Moments

Route

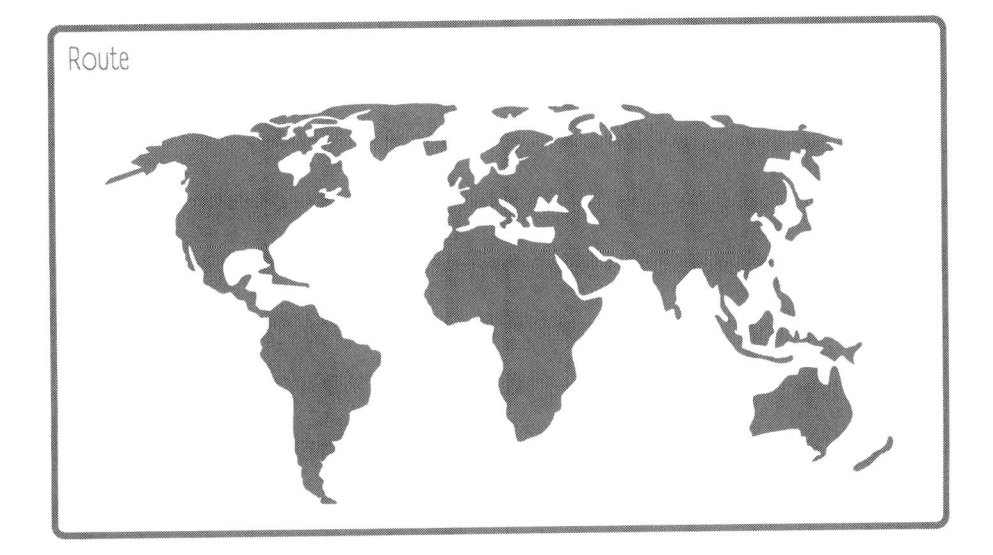

Date:

Departure Location	Departure Time
Stopover	Time
Arrival Location	Date & Time

Weather	
Wind	
Forecast	
Visibility	
Wave	

Course / Coordinates	
Speed	
Distance	
Crew	

Sketch	Notes

Photo

Anecdotes / Special Moments

Route

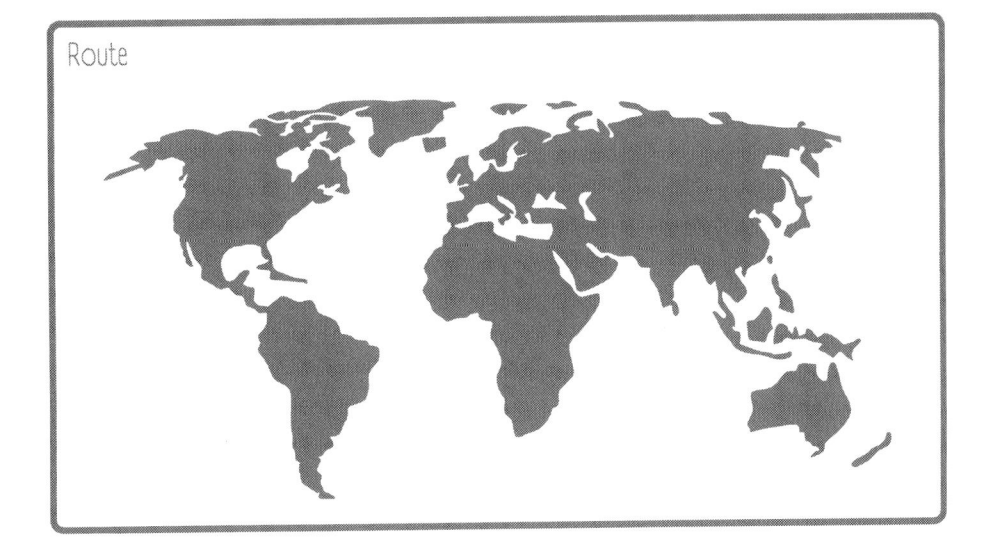

Date:

Departure Location	Departure Time
Stopover	Time
Arrival Location	Date & Time

Weather	
Wind	
Forecast	
Visibility	
Wave	

Course / Coordinates	
Speed	
Distance	
Crew	

Sketch	Notes

Photo

Anecdotes / Special Moments

Route

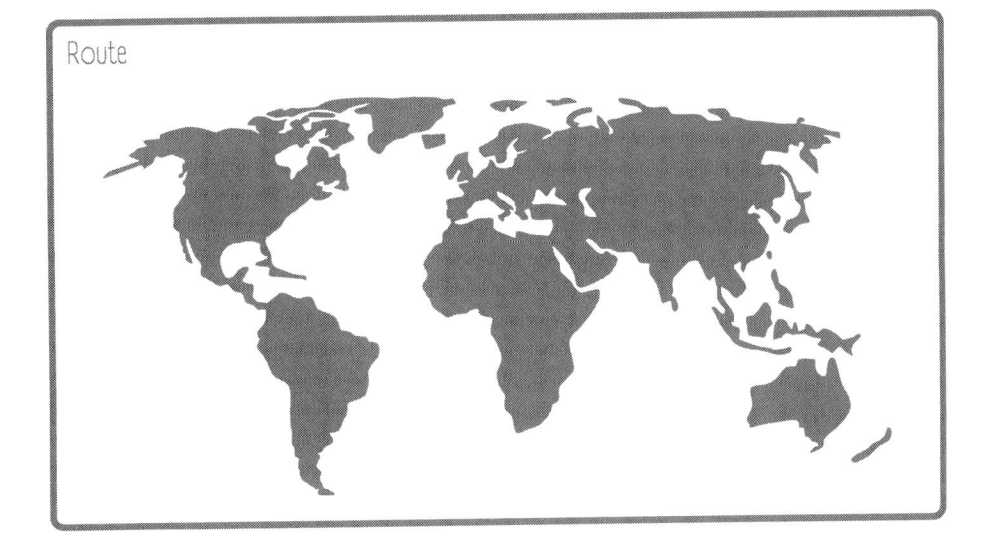

Date: ....

Departure Location	Departure Time
Stopover	Time
Arrival Location	Date & Time

Weather
Wind
Forecast
Visibility
Wave

Course / Coordinates
Speed
Distance
Crew

Sketch	Notes

Photo

Anecdotes / Special Moments

Route

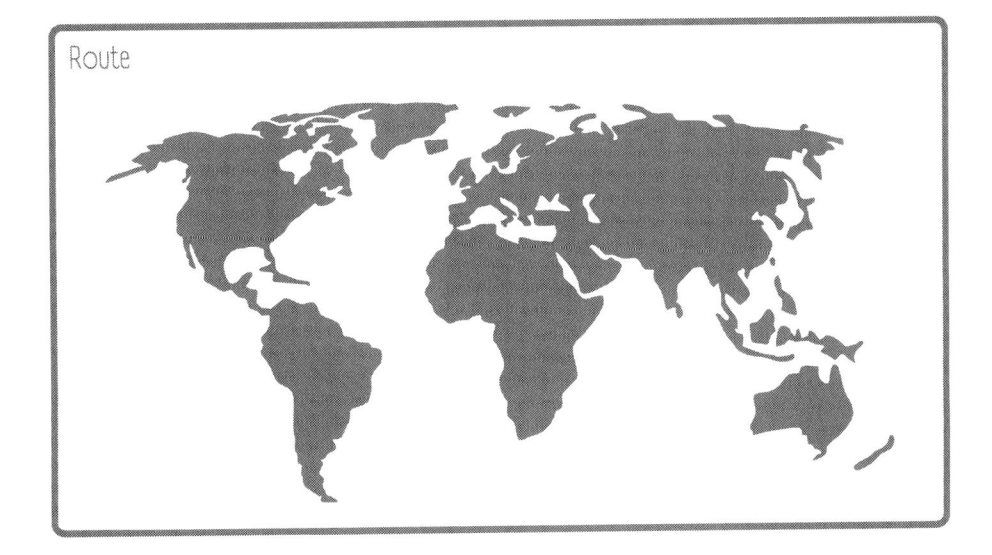

Date:

Departure Location	Departure Time
Stopover	Time
Arrival Location	Date & Time

Weather	
Wind	
Forecast	
Visibility	
Wave	

Course / Coordinates	
Speed	
Distance	
Crew	

Sketch	Notes

Photo

Anecdotes / Special Moments

Route

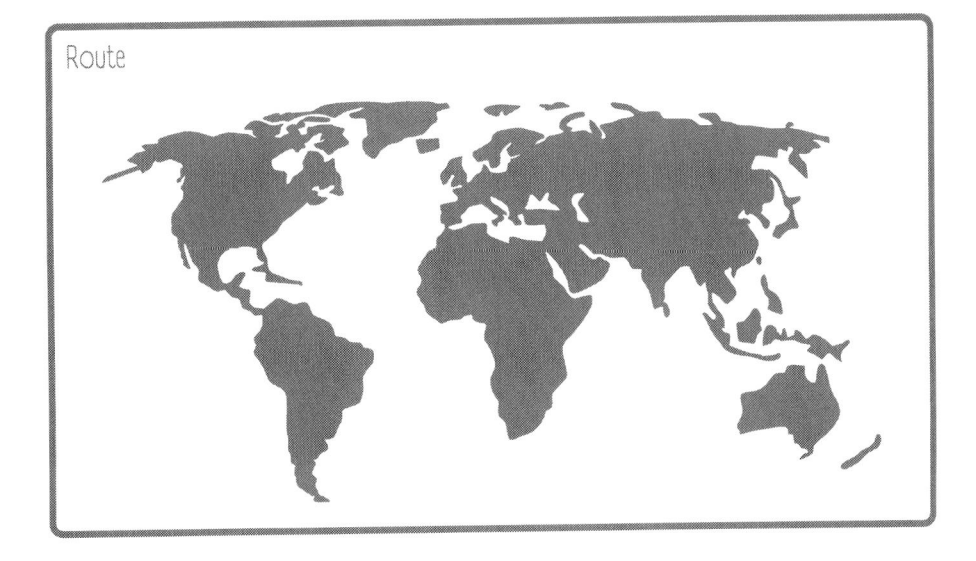

Date:

Departure Location		Departure Time
Stopover		Time
Arrival Location		Date & Time

Weather	
Wind	
Forecast	
Visibility	
Wave	

Course / Coordinates	
Speed	
Distance	
Crew	

Sketch	Notes

Photo

Anecdotes / Special Moments

Route

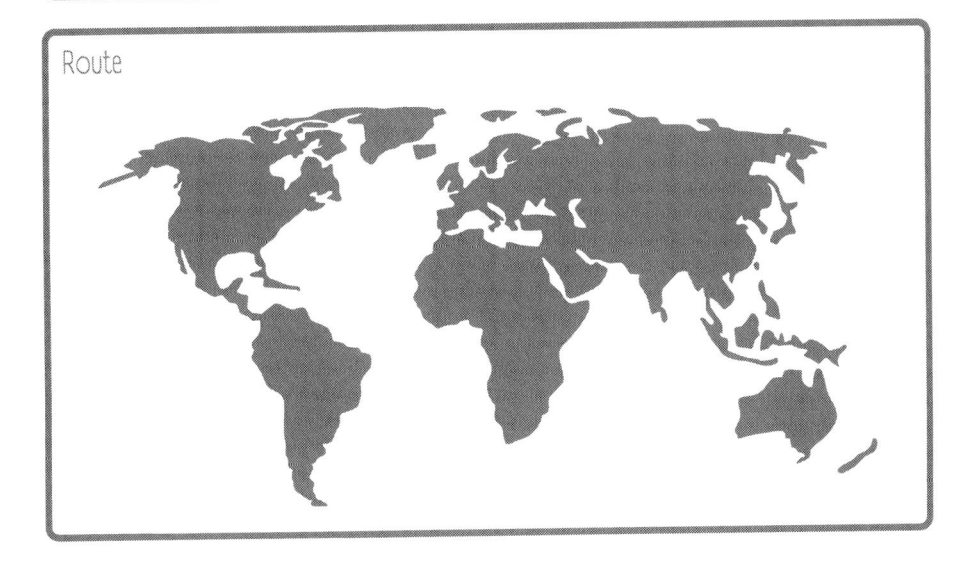

Date: ....

Departure Location	Departure Time
Stopover	Time
Arrival Location	Date & Time

Weather
Wind
Forecast
Visibility
Wave

Course / Coordinates
Speed
Distance
Crew

Sketch	Notes

Photo

Anecdotes / Special Moments

Route

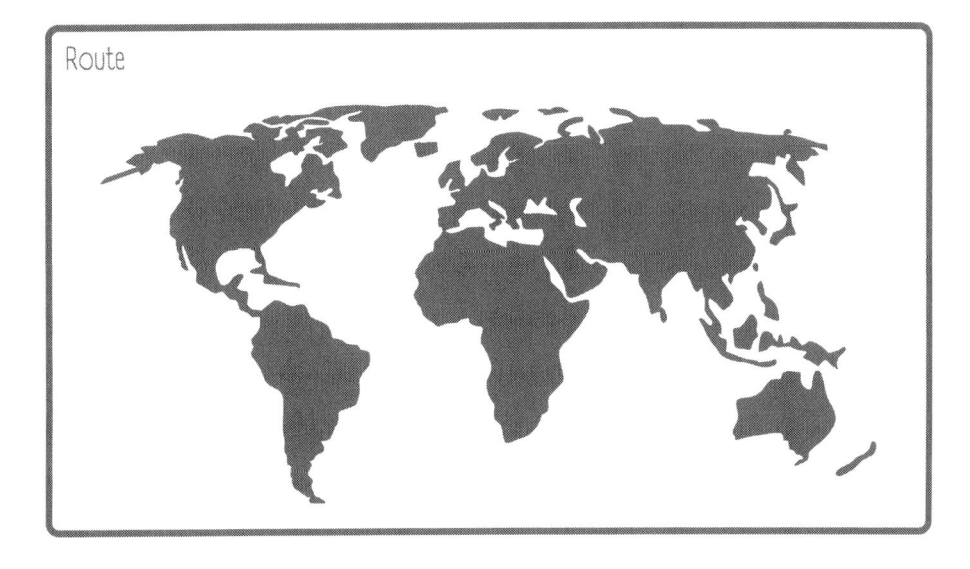

Date:

Departure Location	Departure Time
Stopover	Time
Arrival Location	Date & Time

Weather	
Wind	
Forecast	
Visibility	
Wave	

Course / Coordinates	
Speed	
Distance	
Crew	

Sketch	Notes

Anecdotes / Special Moments

Route

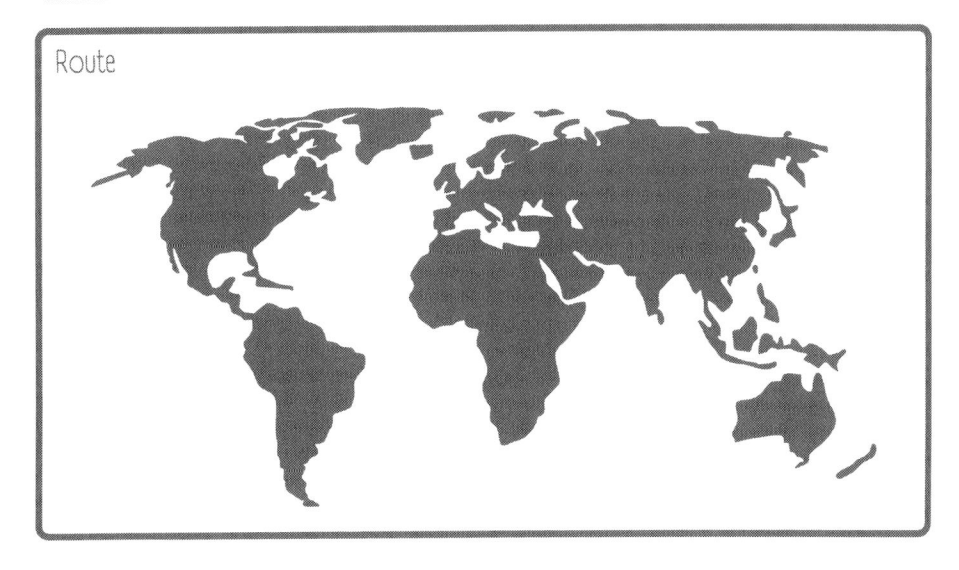

Date: ....

Departure Location	Departure Time
Stopover	Time
Arrival Location	Date & Time

Weather
Wind
Forecast
Visibility
Wave

Course / Coordinates
Speed
Distance
Crew

Sketch	Notes

Photo

Anecdotes / Special Moments

Route

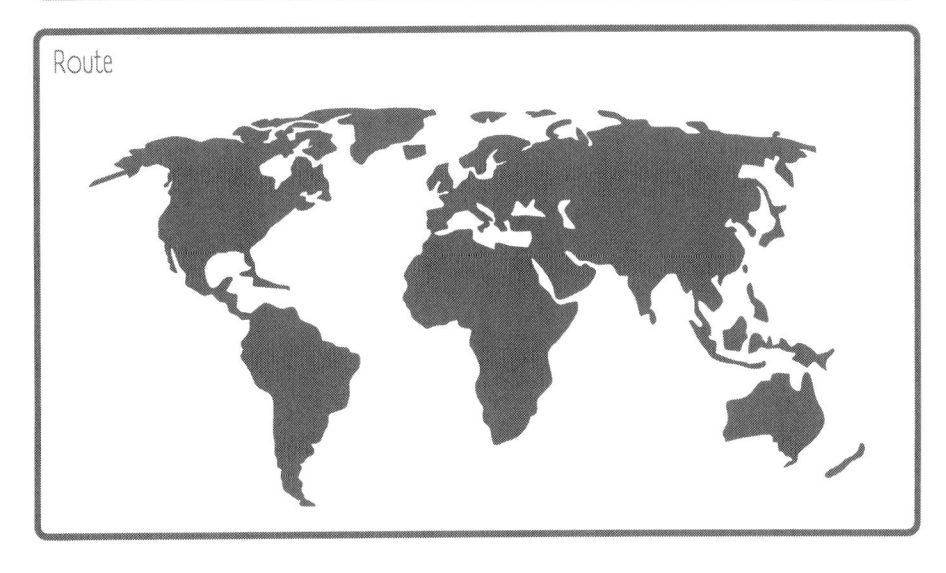

Date: ....

Departure Location	Departure Time
Stopover	Time
Arrival Location	Date & Time

Weather
Wind
Forecast
Visibility
Wave

Course / Coordinates
Speed
Distance
Crew

Sketch	Notes

Photo

Anecdotes / Special Moments

Route

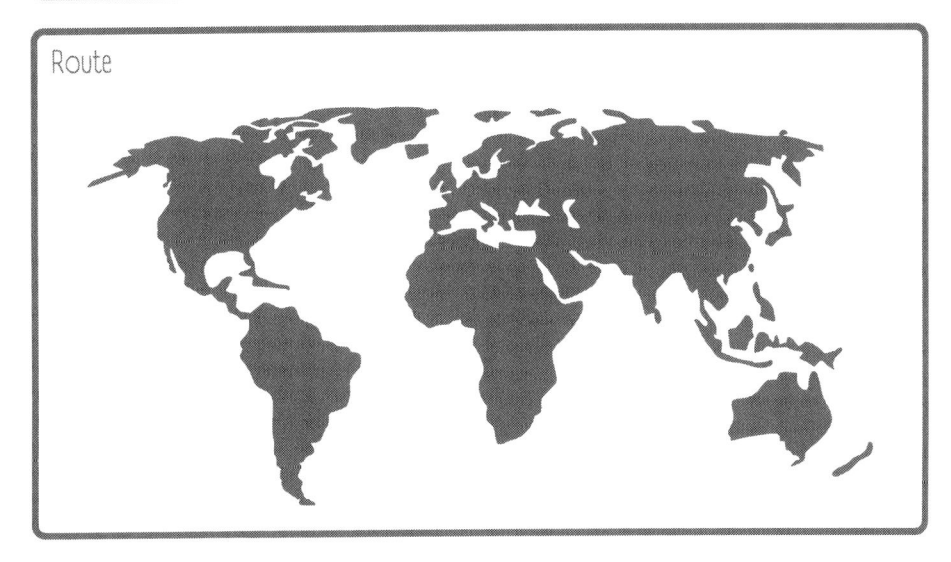

Date:

Departure Location		Departure Time
Stopover		Time
Arrival Location		Date & Time

Weather	
Wind	
Forecast	
Visibility	
Wave	

Course / Coordinates	
Speed	
Distance	
Crew	

Sketch	Notes

Photo

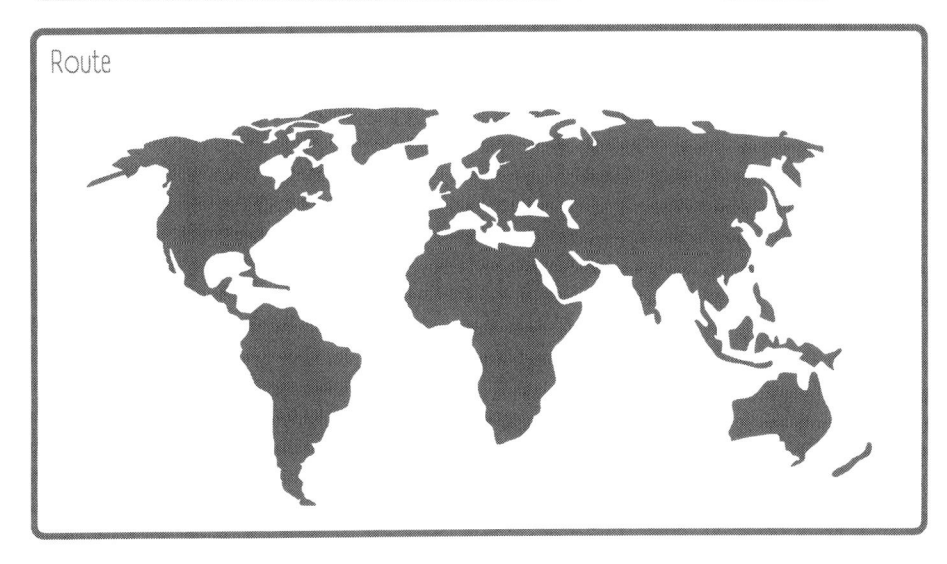

Anecdotes / Special Moments

Route

Date:

Departure Location	Departure Time
Stopover	Time
Arrival Location	Date & Time

Weather
Wind
Forecast
Visibility
Wave

Course / Coordinates
Speed
Distance
Crew

Sketch	Notes

Photo

Anecdotes / Special Moments

Route

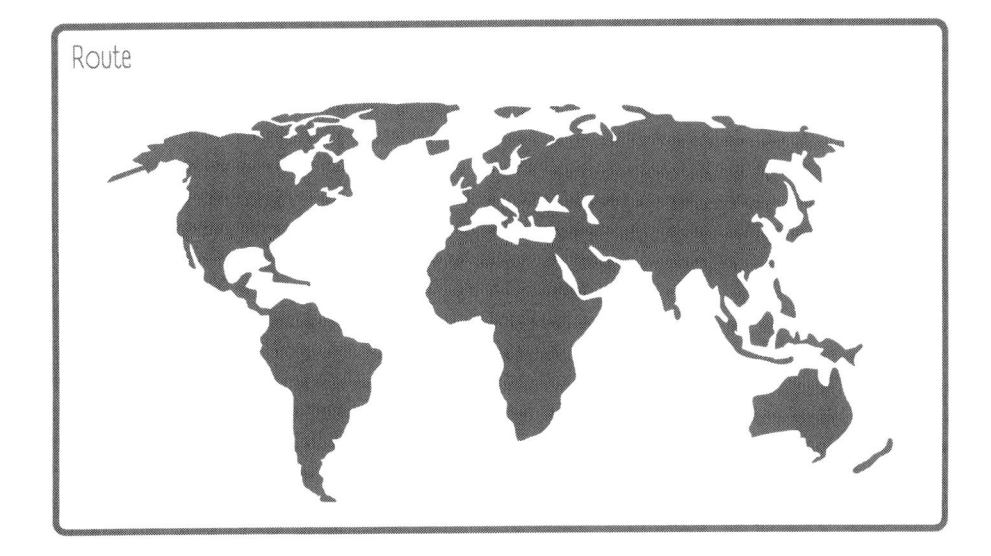

Date:

Departure Location	Departure Time
Stopover	Time
Arrival Location	Date & Time

Weather
Wind
Forecast
Visibility
Wave

Course / Coordinates
Speed
Distance
Crew

Sketch	Notes

Photo

Anecdotes / Special Moments

Route

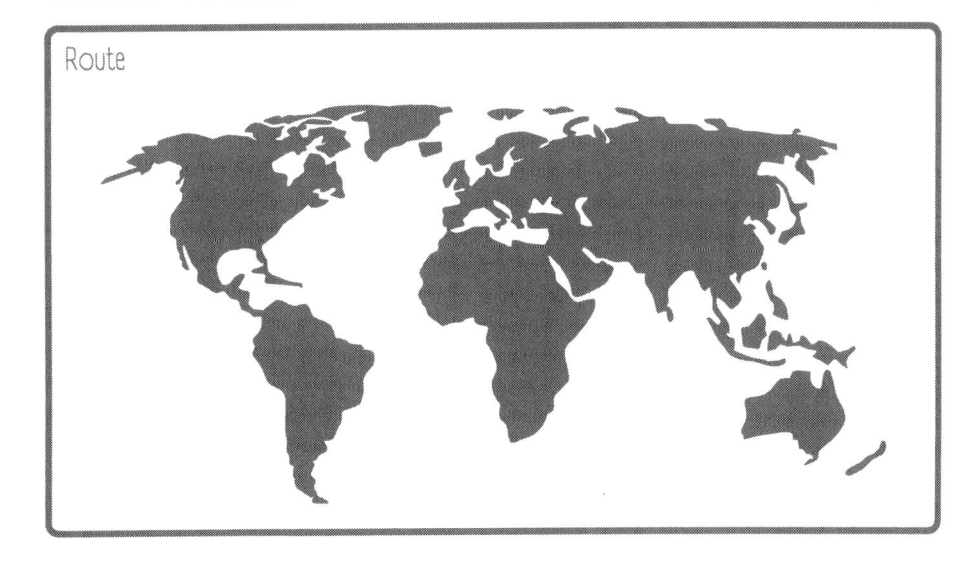

Date: _____

Departure Location	Departure Time
Stopover	Time
Arrival Location	Date & Time

Weather
Wind
Forecast
Visibility
Wave

Course / Coordinates
Speed
Distance
Crew

Sketch	Notes

Photo

Anecdotes / Special Moments

Route

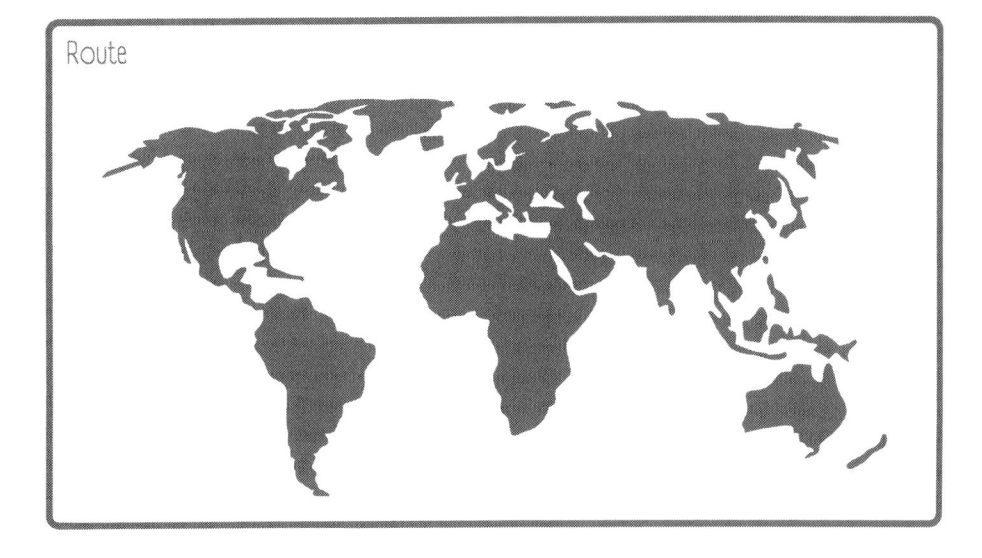

Date: ....

Departure Location	Departure Time
Stopover	Time
Arrival Location	Date & Time

Weather	
Wind	
Forecast	
Visibility	
Wave	

Course / Coordinates	
Speed	
Distance	
Crew	

Sketch	Notes

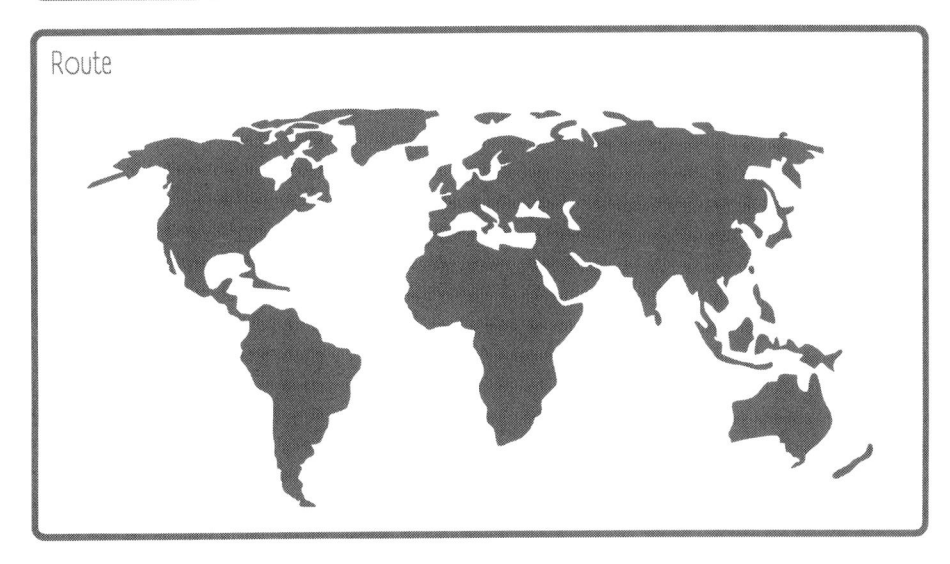

Photo

Anecdotes / Special Moments

Route

Date:

Departure Location	Departure Time
Stopover	Time
Arrival Location	Date & Time

Weather
Wind
Forecast
Visibility
Wave

Course / Coordinates
Speed
Distance
Crew

Sketch	Notes

Photo

Anecdotes / Special Moments

Route

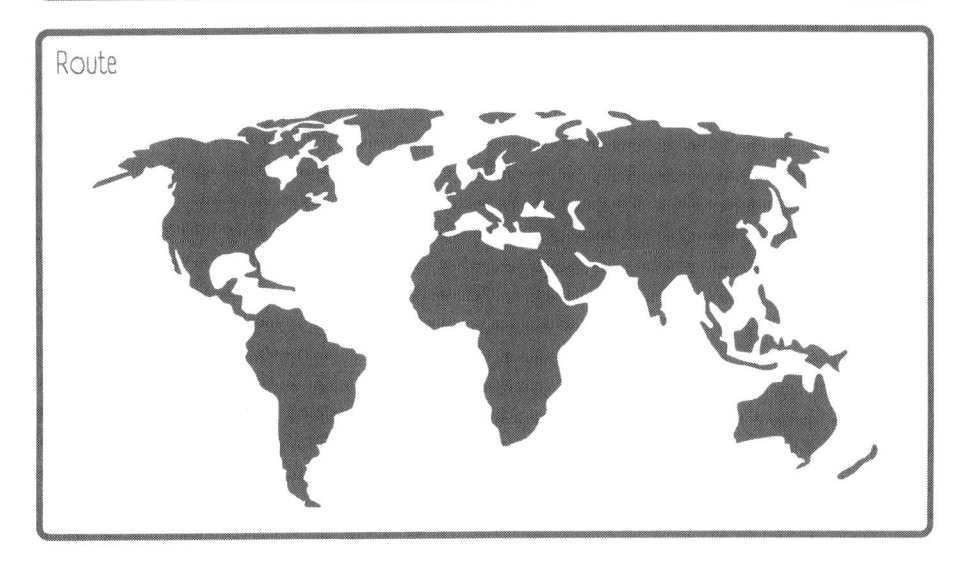

Date: ....

Departure Location	Departure Time
Stopover	Time
Arrival Location	Date & Time

Weather
Wind
Forecast
Visibility
Wave

Course / Coordinates
Speed
Distance
Crew

Sketch	Notes

Photo

Anecdotes / Special Moments

Route

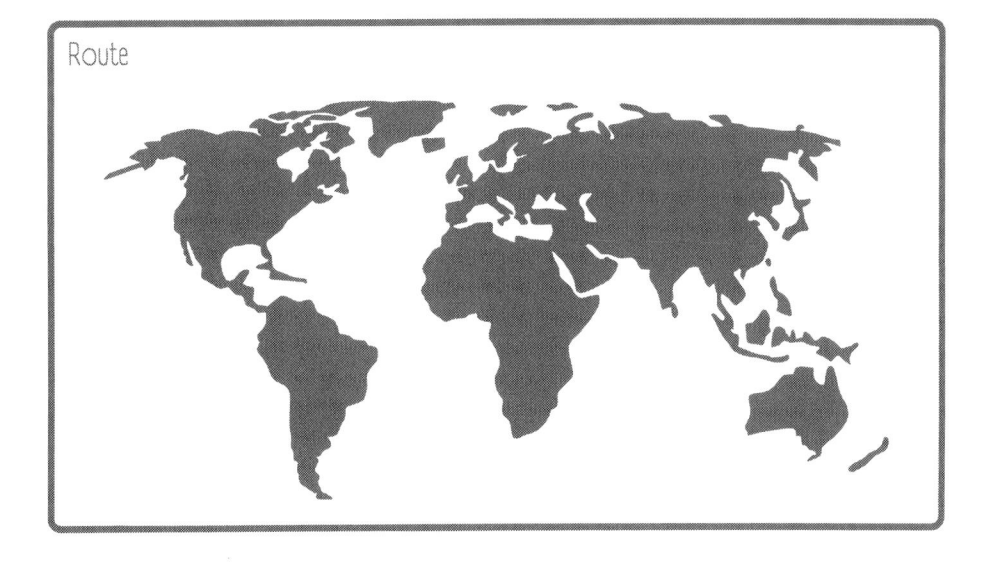

Date: ....

Departure Location	Departure Time
Stopover	Time
Arrival Location	Date & Time

Weather
Wind
Forecast
Visibility
Wave

Course / Coordinates
Speed
Distance
Crew

Sketch	Notes

Anecdotes / Special Moments

Route

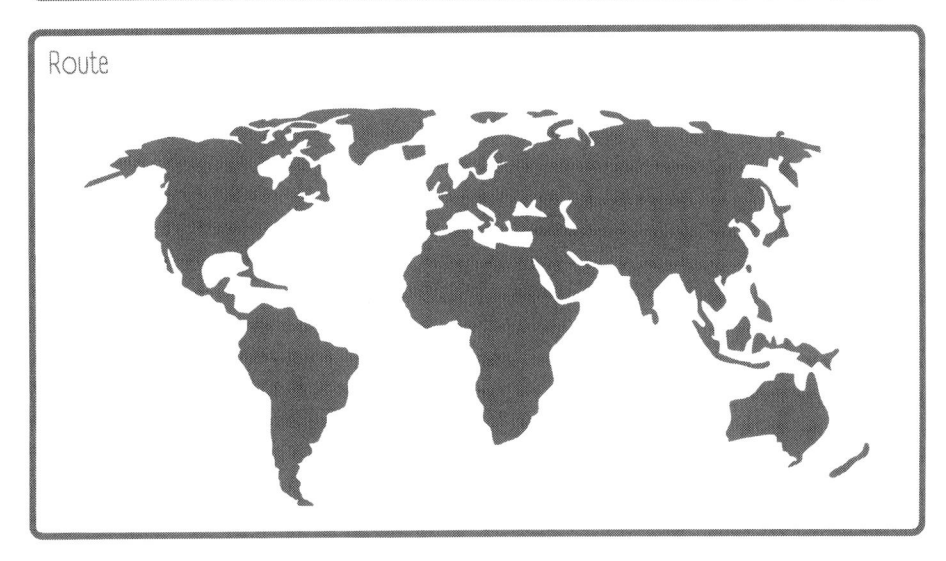

Date: ....

Departure Location	Departure Time
Stopover	Time
Arrival Location	Date & Time

Weather
Wind
Forecast
Visibility
Wave

Course / Coordinates
Speed
Distance
Crew

Sketch	Notes

Photo

Anecdotes / Special Moments

Route

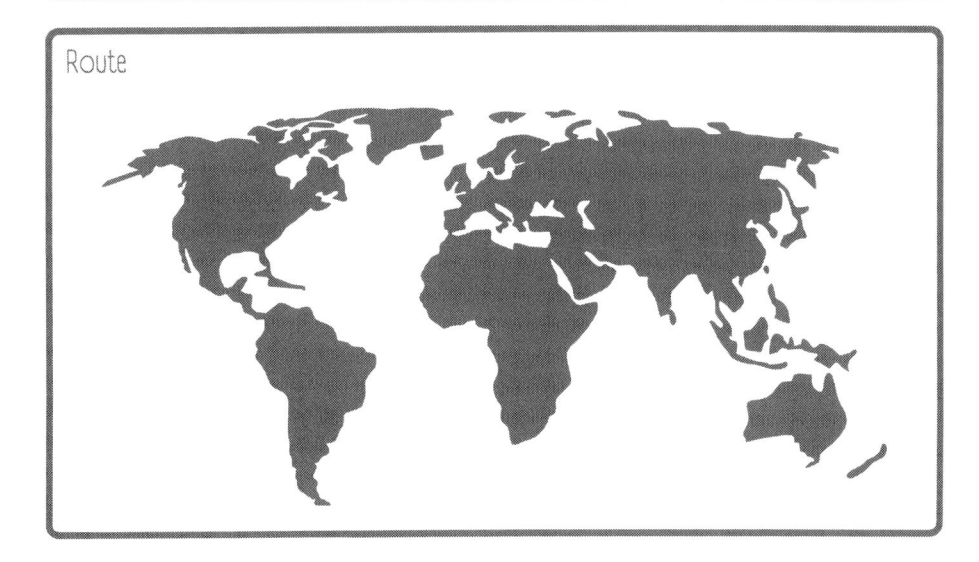

Date:

Departure Location	Departure Time
Stopover	Time
Arrival Location	Date & Time

Weather
Wind
Forecast
Visibility
Wave

Course / Coordinates
Speed
Distance
Crew

Sketch	Notes

Photo

Anecdotes / Special Moments

Route

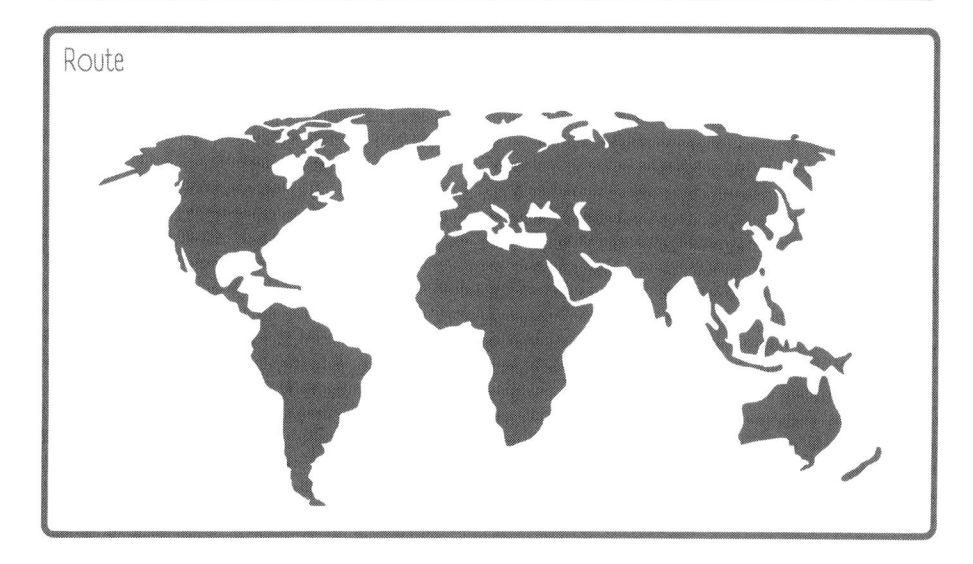

Date:

Departure Location	Departure Time
Stopover	Time
Arrival Location	Date & Time

Weather
Wind
Forecast
Visibility
Wave

Course / Coordinates
Speed
Distance
Crew

Sketch	Notes

Photo

Anecdotes / Special Moments

Route

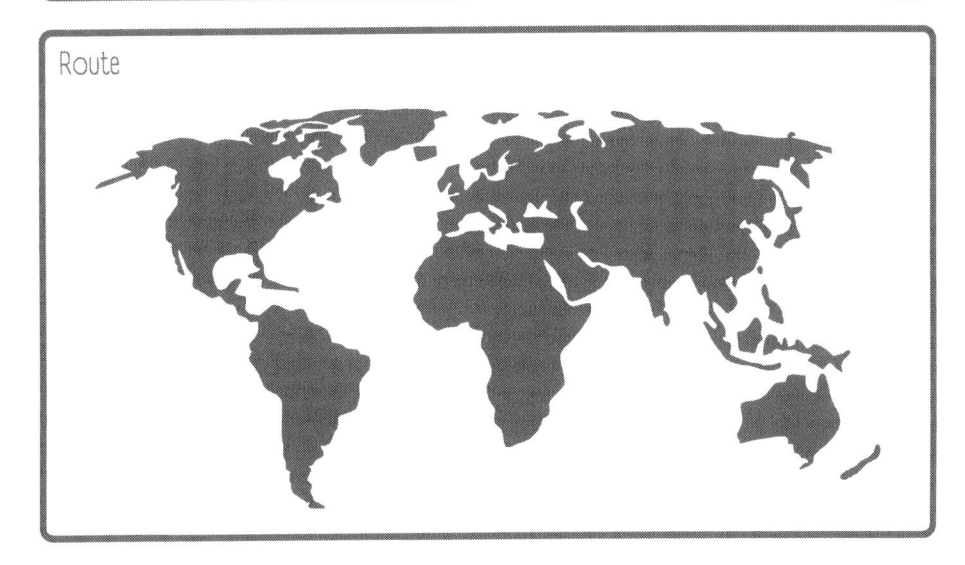

Date:

Departure Location	Departure Time
Stopover	Time
Arrival Location	Date & Time

Weather	
Wind	
Forecast	
Visibility	
Wave	

Course / Coordinates	
Speed	
Distance	
Crew	

Sketch	Notes

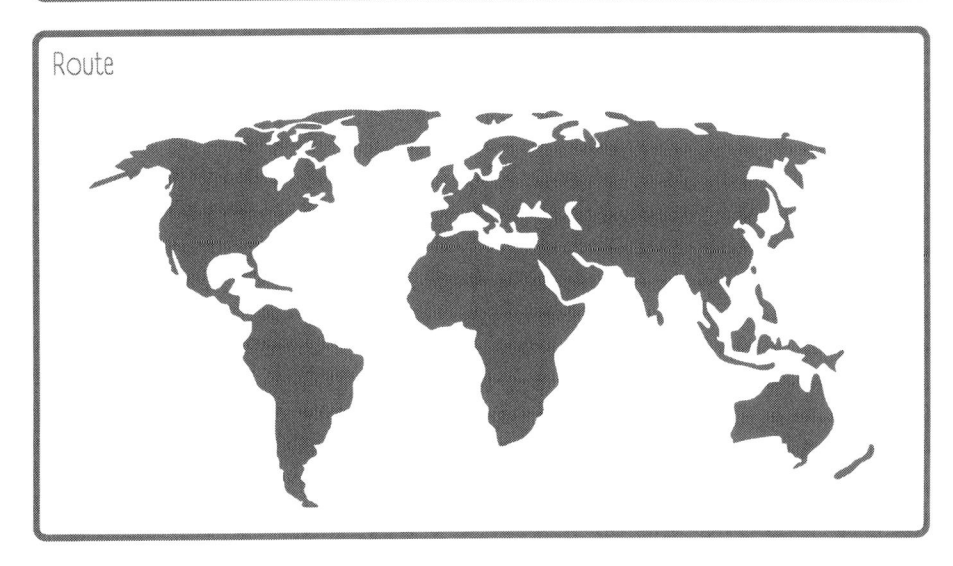

Date: ....

Departure Location	Departure Time
Stopover	Time
Arrival Location	Date & Time

Weather
Wind
Forecast
Visibility
Wave

Course / Coordinates
Speed
Distance
Crew

Sketch	Notes

Anecdotes / Special Moments

Route

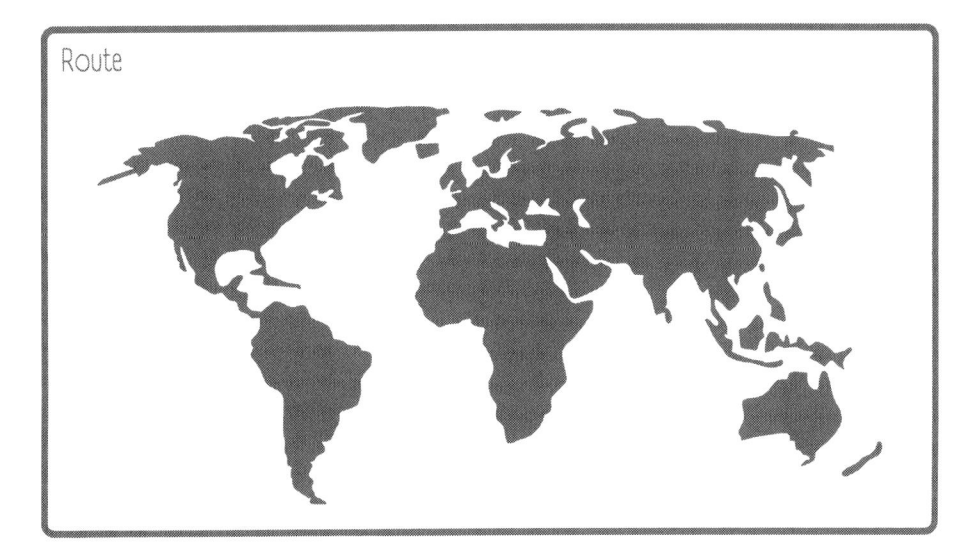

Date:

Departure Location	Departure Time
Stopover	Time
Arrival Location	Date & Time

Weather
Wind
Forecast
Visibility
Wave

Course / Coordinates
Speed
Distance
Crew

Sketch	Notes

Photo

Anecdotes / Special Moments

Route

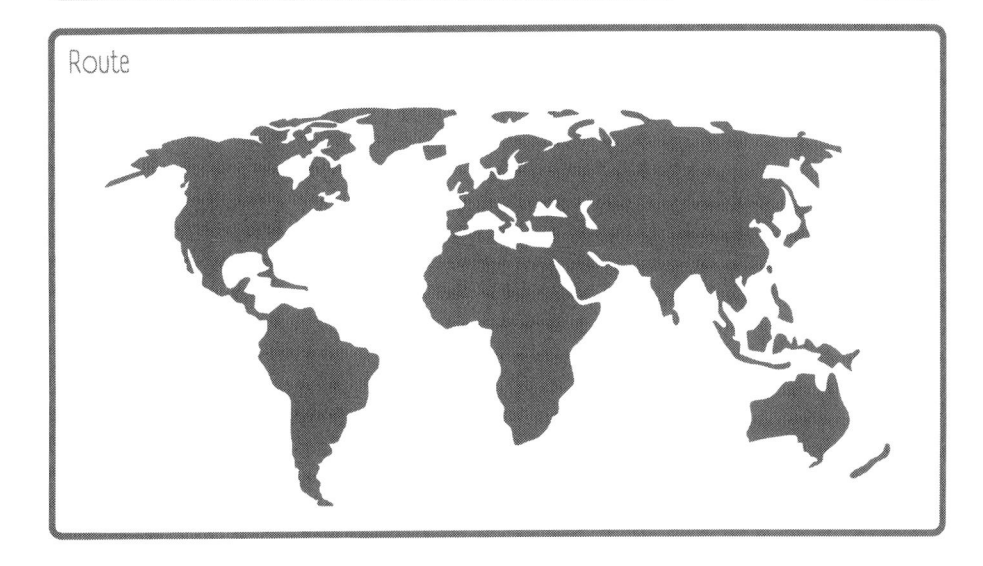

Date:

Departure Location	Departure Time
Stopover	Time
Arrival Location	Date & Time

Weather	
Wind	
Forecast	
Visibility	
Wave	

Course / Coordinates	
Speed	
Distance	
Crew	

Sketch	Notes

Photo

Anecdotes / Special Moments

Route

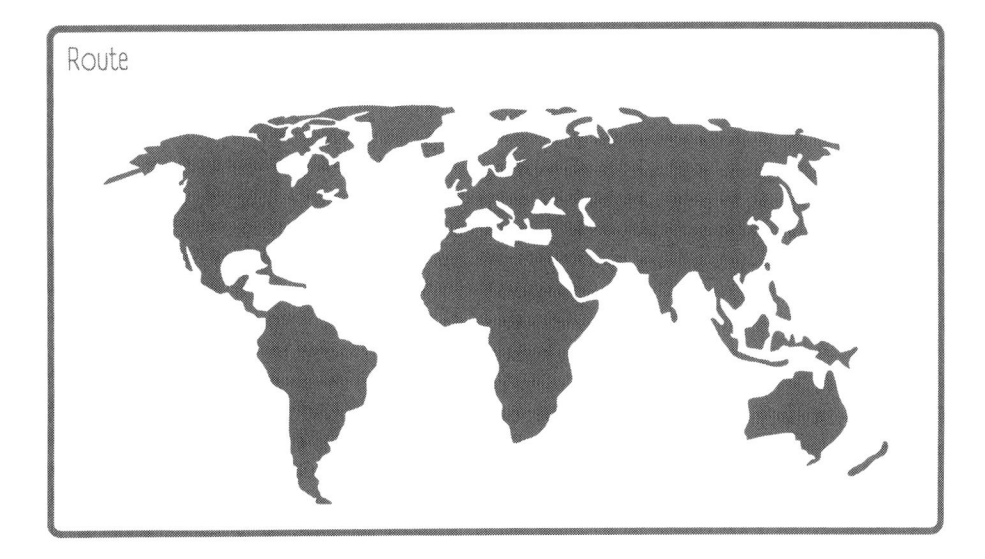

Date: ....

Departure Location	Departure Time
Stopover	Time
Arrival Location	Date & Time

Weather
Wind
Forecast
Visibility
Wave

Course / Coordinates
Speed
Distance
Crew

Sketch	Notes

Photo

Anecdotes / Special Moments

Route

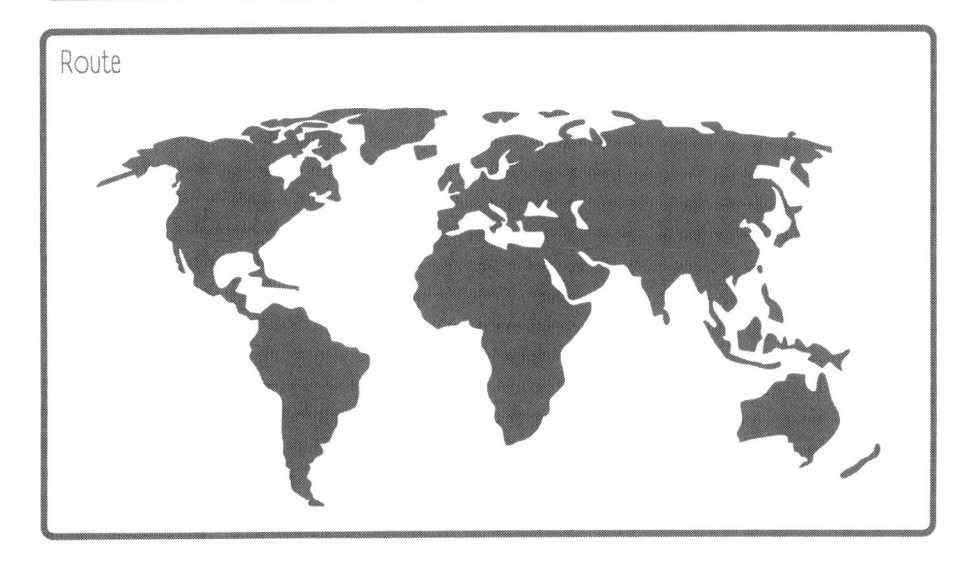

Date:

Departure Location	Departure Time
Stopover	Time
Arrival Location	Date & Time

Weather	
Wind	
Forecast	
Visibility	
Wave	

Course / Coordinates	
Speed	
Distance	
Crew	

Sketch	Notes

Photo

Anecdotes / Special Moments

Route

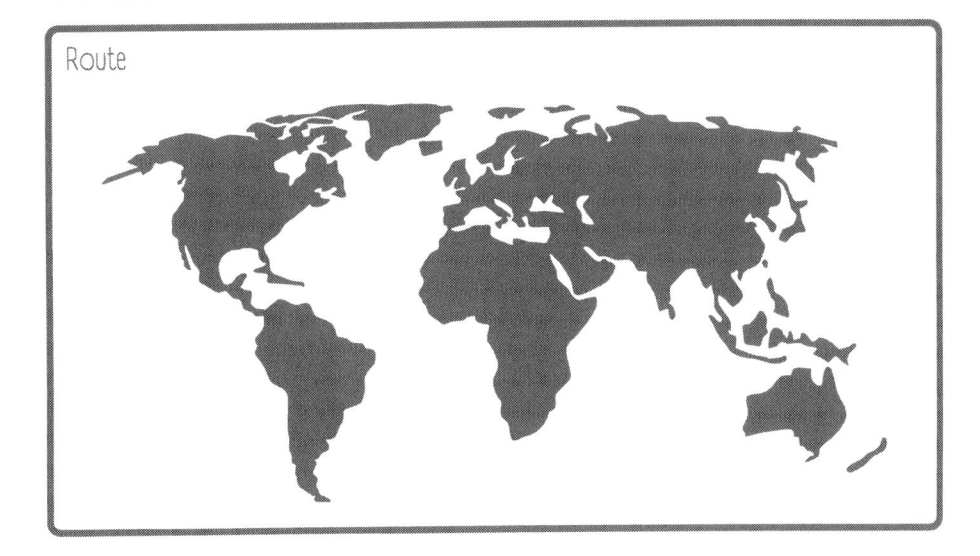

Date:

Departure Location	Departure Time
Stopover	Time
Arrival Location	Date & Time

Weather
Wind
Forecast
Visibility
Wave

Course / Coordinates
Speed
Distance
Crew

Sketch	Notes

Anecdotes / Special Moments

Route

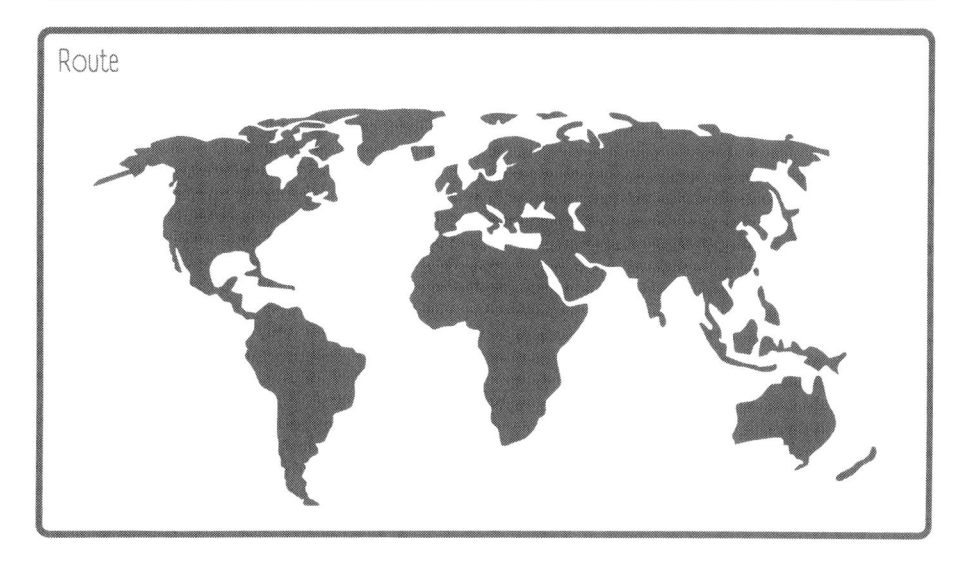

Date: ....

Departure Location	Departure Time
Stopover	Time
Arrival Location	Date & Time

Weather
Wind
Forecast
Visibility
Wave

Course / Coordinates
Speed
Distance
Crew

Sketch	Notes

Photo

Anecdotes / Special Moments

Route

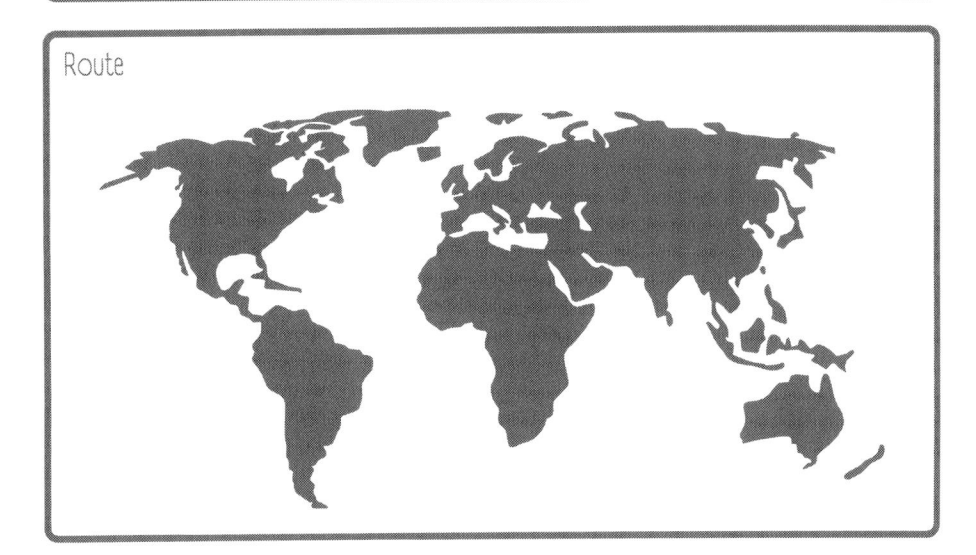

Date:

Departure Location	Departure Time
Stopover	Time
Arrival Location	Date & Time

Weather
Wind
Forecast
Visibility
Wave

Course / Coordinates
Speed
Distance
Crew

Sketch	Notes

Photo

Anecdotes / Special Moments

Route

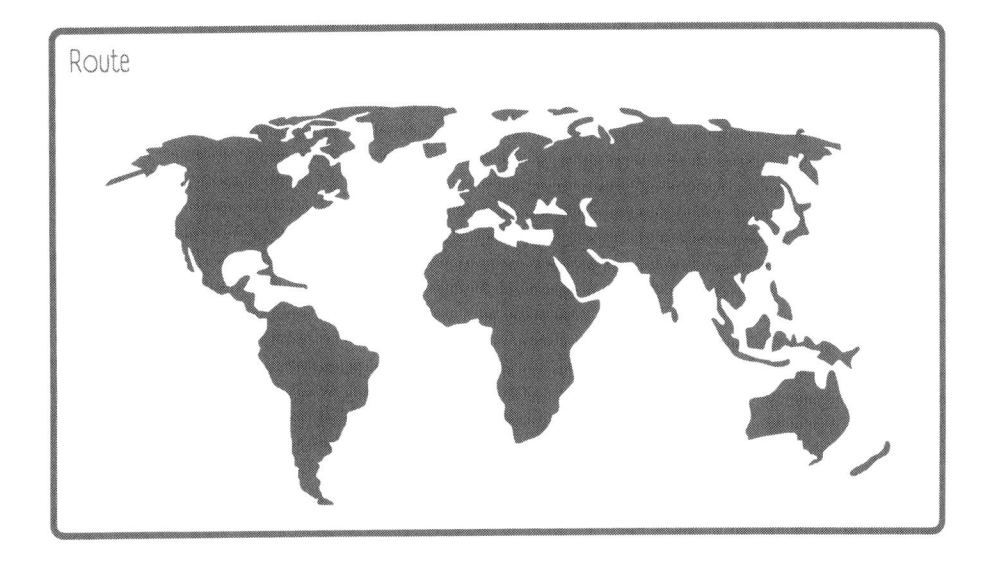

Printed in Great Britain
by Amazon